Conservation

Sylvia Earle
Ocean Explorer

Dennis Fertig

Heinemann
LIBRARY

Chicago, Illinois

© 2015 Heinemann Library,
an imprint of Capstone Global Library, LLC
Chicago, Illinois

To contact Capstone Global Library please call
800-747-4992, or visit our web site
www.capstonepub.com

Edited by Clare Lewis, Abby Colich, Diyan Leake,
and Brynn Baker
Designed by Philippa Jenkins and Kyle Grenz
Original illustrations © Capstone Global Library
Ltd 2014
Illustrated by HL Studios
Picture research by Tracy Cummins
Production by Victoria Fitzgerald
Originated by Capstone Global Library Ltd
Printed and bound in China by CTPS

Library of Congress Cataloging-in-Publication Data
Fertig, Dennis
Sylvia Earle: Ocean Explorer (Women in Conservation)
Cataloging-in-Publication Data is available at the
Library of Congress website.

ISBN 978-1-4846-0470-0 (hardcover)
ISBN 978-1-4846-0475-5 (paperback)
ISBN 978-1-4846-0485-4 (eBook PDF)

18 17 16 15 14
10 9 8 7 6 5 4 3 2 1

Acknowledgments
We would like to thank the following for permission
to reproduce photographs: Al Giddings Images Inc.:
Al Giddings, 26, 31; Alamy: © AF archive, 11, © Mark
Conlin, 24; Corbis: © Bettmann, 9, 20, 29, © Macduff
Everton, 43, © Roger Ressmeyer, 33, © Stephen Frink,
34; Flickr: Duke University Archives, 13; Getty Images:
Alex Wong, 41, Mark Conlin, 25, National Geographic/
Pierre Mion, 16; Kip Evans: front cover; National
Geogrpahic: BATES LITTLEHALES, 23, NATALIE B.
FOBES, 36, Wolcott Henry, 5; newscom: Erik Hill/
Anchorage Daily News/MCT, 37; NOAA: 19, Historic
Fisheries Collection, 14, OAR/National Undersea
Research Program (NURP), 28, 39, UNCW, 12;
Shutterstock: AppalachianViews, 6, Kristina Vackova,
8, Nantawat Chotsuwan, 10, Rich Carey, 4;
Wikimedia: NOAA, 38

We would like to thank Michael Bright for his
invaluable help in the preparation of this book.

007009CTPSF14

Contents

Some words are printed in bold, **like this**. You can find out what they mean by looking in the glossary on page 45.

Who Is Sylvia Earle?

When Sylvia Earle was 12 years old, her family moved to a house in Florida by the Gulf of Mexico. Earle had no idea then how important the Gulf would become to her. Quickly, she learned.

By age 13, Earle used swimming goggles to explore the Gulf's warm waters. At age 16, she wore a diving helmet and reached the deep bottom of a river near the Gulf. A year later, she learned to **scuba dive**. This allowed her to discover the Gulf's undersea secrets and, eventually, the secrets of the world's oceans.

Earle's dives were always about adventure, but they grew to be much more. Earle was a curious student of the seas—a natural scientist.

Sylvia Earle has spent her lifetime exploring the hidden beauty, wonder, and secrets of the undersea world.

"Her Deepness"

Earle grew up to be a **marine botanist**. She worked hard to learn everything she could about ocean life. She bravely explored ocean depths that others could not reach, and she often discovered things that others had not seen. Along the way, Earle realized she had a talent for explaining complicated scientific information to the public. She was able to inspire people to value and protect the oceans.

Sylvia Earle was among the first marine scientists to routinely scuba dive for research.

Nearly 80 years old in 2014, Earle has spent more than 7,000 hours exploring ocean depths. She continued to find ways to go deeper and deeper. Earle formed companies to make sea crafts able to reach greater depths than ever before. She has also led numerous scientific teams in explorations around the world.

Most importantly, Earle has proven to the world that Earth's survival depends on the health of its oceans. Her diving bravery has earned her the nickname, "Her Deepness." However, her work to protect Earth's vital resources have earned her an even more fitting title, "Hero of the Planet."

What Inspired Earle?

Sylvia Earle was born in 1935. Her father, Lewis, was a handyman and an electrician. When the family bought an old farmhouse near Paulsboro, New Jersey, he installed electricity and modern plumbing. Later Lewis worked nights at a factory so that he could enjoy his days outside with Earle and her two brothers.

Earle's mother, Alice, was known locally as "the Bird Lady" for helping injured animals. She loved nature in all of its details. Alice shared that love with her children.

Young Earle's first ocean adventures took place on New Jersey's Atlantic coast.

Living fearlessly in nature

Earle's parents inspired her to live fearlessly. During beach outings, young Earle toddled around, studying and picking up fearsome-looking horseshoe crabs. On one particular visit, a wave suddenly knocked tiny Earle over. Her mother was delighted as Earle jumped up unafraid and ran into the next wave. Later, at age five, brave Earle did not hesitate to fly as the only passenger on a tiny Piper airplane.

In Her Own Words

Earle remembers:

"My first encounter with the ocean was on the Jersey Shore when I was three years old and I got knocked down by a wave. The ocean certainly got my attention! It wasn't frightening. It was exhilarating! And since then, life in the ocean has captured my imagination and held it ever since."

Earle was naturally curious. She collected plant, rock, and bug **specimens** to study, just as scientists do. Earle's mother called these, "Sylvia's investigations." Earle patiently observed nature on her family's farm and in a nearby pond. She took notes and made drawings of her observations.

Living on a farm, Earle and her brothers shared many pets, including a horse named Tony. She loved being surrounded by so many animals.

A bad move?

When Earle was 12, her family moved to Dunedin, Florida. Earle missed the farm, but she discovered that her new home offered exciting new adventures. Earle's backyard ended at the waters of the Gulf of Mexico. When Earle's parents gave her swimming goggles for her 13th birthday, those waters changed her life.

Earle swam well and loved it. Her "investigations" now took her under the water. Sea horses were one of her first discoveries. They sadly reminded her of her horse, Tony. But they also symbolized the amazing new world she was exploring.

It is easy to see why the sea horse reminded Earle of Tony.

William Beebe (right) and Otis Barton (left) stand next to their bathysphere.

New discoveries—good and bad

Not all of Earle's discoveries were delightful. During an underwater swim in the sea, Earle and a friend witnessed an orange mass of something being pumped from a long pipe into the clear-blue waters. It was waste from an orange juice factory. That was one of the milder ocean **pollutants** Earle would eventually discover.

Earle's investigations also included exploring Dunedin's library shelves. Her favorite books had vivid descriptions of oceans and adventures within them. Authors Rachel Carson and Jacques Cousteau wrote of the inviting wonders under the seas. William Beebe, her favorite writer, shared real-life adventures that inspired Earle in her own life.

William Beebe

William Beebe was a scientist, explorer, and inventor. With Otis Barton, he developed the bathysphere. This large, metal ball allowed scientists to safely travel to the depths of the oceans.

In 1934 Beebe and Barton dove 3,028 feet (923 meters) under the sea. At that depth—the deepest any human had gone and survived—they saw wonders that would later inspire Earle and others to make their own ocean plunges.

Deeper into the sea

In 1952 Earle graduated from high school at age 16. That year she made her first breathing-assisted underwater dive in a deep river near the ocean. She wore a heavy metal helmet. A long hose connected her helmet to a machine that squeezed regular air into **compressed air**. Compressed air withstands the heavy pressure that deep water puts on the human body.

When Earle had descended 30 feet (9 meters) to the river's bottom, a sharp-toothed fish called an alligator gar approached her. It did not frighten Earle. But later she was scared by a sudden attack of dizziness. She quickly tugged on the hose to signal trouble and started back up to the surface.

Some alligator gars can grow to be 10 feet (3 meters) long.

On shore, Earle learned that the machine had been feeding her compressed air *and* fuel fumes. The fumes almost killed her. But that did not stop her from diving again. In fact, this dive reinforced Earle's career goal of teaching **marine biology**, the study of life under the ocean.

Scuba diving

That summer, Earle took a class in marine biology taught by Dr. Harold Humm. Humm encouraged students to learn scuba diving, something developed by Jacques Cousteau a decade earlier. Earle loved scuba diving so much that she eventually changed her mind. Instead of teaching, Earle would explore ocean depths. She eventually helped **pioneer** scuba diving as a **marine** scientist's favorite exploration tool.

Jacques Cousteau

Jacques Cousteau was an explorer, scientist, and writer. He produced films and TV programs that detailed his underwater explorations. His work inspired great curiosity about the world under the sea.

Jacques Cousteau's long life of underwater exploration helped inspire Sylvia Earle.

How Did Earle's Career Begin?

Becoming a scientist requires time, research, and college degrees. Sylvia Earle earned her first degree, called a bachelor's degree, in 1955 from Florida State University.

The next year, Earle earned her second, called a master's degree, from Duke University in North Carolina. There, Earle focused her studies on marine botany. She was especially interested in **algae**. Earle spent several years researching algae before earning her final degree, called a doctorate, from Duke in 1966.

After earning her master's degree, Earle married Jack Taylor, a **zoologist**. Over the next few years, they had two children. During this busy time, Earle continued her research on types of algae.

DID YOU KNOW?

All types of algae grow in water. Some algae are large like seaweed. Other types are only visible through a microscope. Although algae appear plantlike, they are not plants. They are a simple form of life called protists. Life on earth needs algae. Through **photosynthesis**, algae are oxygen-making machines that keep us breathing. They are also vital parts of the ocean **food chain**.

Scientist and teacher, Dr. Harold Humm (in water), taught students how to use scuba equipment to study ocean life.

Exploring the Indian Ocean

In 1964 a scientific research ship called the *Anton Bruun* began a six week **expedition** in the Indian Ocean. The ship needed a marine botanist. Earle took the position and became the only woman among the ship's 70-member crew. In the 1960s, that meant she was not welcomed by everyone. Some men doubted women's abilities. Journalists even wrote stories about Earle's groundbreaking role.

Earle proved extremely capable. She became the ship's spokesperson in ports along the coast of Africa and nearby islands. More importantly, Earle spent long hours doing research in the magical undersea world she loved. Earle then spent long nights writing notes about what she had seen and learned during the day.

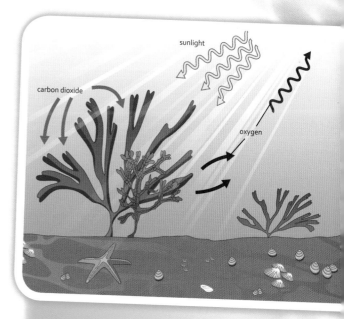

sunlight

carbon dioxide

oxygen

All plants convert **carbon dioxide** into oxygen and sugar using energy from the sun. The sugar is used in the seaweed's cells to provide energy for growth. Oxygen is released into the water and air, sustaining life.

More voyages

Earle made more voyages aboard the *Anton Bruun*. On a 1965 Pacific Ocean trip, she discovered an unknown variety of umbrella-shaped algae deep within the sea. She named it *Hummbrella hydra*, in honor of Harold Humm.

Before its life as a science ship, the *Anton Bruun* was a Navy gunboat called the *Williamsburg*.

Earle was well suited to become the chief scientist aboard the *Anton Bruun*. But that opportunity was not offered to women. Earle would soon make her own opportunities, perhaps inspired by another female scientist, Eugenie Clark.

Eugenie Clark

Clark was an **ichthyologist** who studied sharks. She was also a scuba-diving pioneer. Clark introduced Earle to a broader view of ocean ecology. Clark studied the relationship of living things in the ocean to their environment and to one another. Clark founded Cape Haze Marine Laboratory, now called Mote Marine Laboratory, in Florida. She eventually appointed Earle its resident director, which meant Earle led the laboratory's team of marine scientists.

Clark was also a wife and mother. She understood the strain that Earle faced balancing family life with serious scientific research. That strain led to Earle's divorce from her first husband. Later, she met and married Giles Mead, a leading ichthyologist at Harvard University.

Deep Diver

In 1968 Earle took her first underwater ride aboard a tiny **submersible** called *Deep Diver*. After a 20-minute, 125-foot (38-meter) plunge, Earle exited the submersible and explored the ocean's floor for 90 minutes. It was her longest time underwater to date.

DID YOU KNOW?

A submersible is a craft designed to work deep under the sea. Submersibles are usually **tethered** to either another ship or a platform above the water. They are built to withstand the heavy pressure of the seawater. Some submersibles carry research equipment, but others carry one or two people and require a breathing system. Submersibles allow scientists to explore even deeper into the seas.

What Made Earle Famous?

In 1969 the U.S. government began a **saturation dive** project in an underwater laboratory called **Tektite**. Saturation dives are long-term stays underwater that allow divers' bodies to more easily recover from undersea exploration.

The first dive involved a team of four male scientists. They spent four months in a **habitat** 50 feet (15 meters) under the ocean water near the Virgin Islands. The project's goal was to learn how humans survived in a small underwater home.

An illustration shows the Tektite II team exploring outside the habitat.

Women and Tektite

More underwater projects for Tektite II were planned for 1970. Each project would allow participating scientists to conduct undersea studies of their own. Scientists were asked to volunteer.

Earle applied, hoping to expand her algae studies. She quickly discovered a problem. Tektite officials did not expect female scientists to apply! When women did apply, officials did not know how to react. They had made no plans for men and women to live underwater together.

Eventually, officials decided to form a team of women scientists to live together underwater for two weeks, the length of most Tektite II projects. The team included Earle.

DID YOU KNOW?

Tektites are small, glass-like rocks formed when meteorites (pieces of rock or metal from space) crash onto Earth. They are often discovered in oceans. Tektite was a good name for the habitat project. Both space and ocean scientists planned the project to study how groups of people work together and thrive while living in small, close quarters for a long time. They were also interested in learning how new breathing devices helped explorers survive in challenging airless environments such as oceans or space. What scientists learned helped both astronauts and **aquanauts**.

Leading the team

By now Earle had been doing serious scientific research for more than a decade. Her extensive algae study had been published and earned great respect in the scientific world. She had spent two years leading Clark's research lab. Earle had more than 1,000 hours of diving experience. She had been an effective spokesperson for various projects. Earle was fearless. There was no question, Dr. Sylvia Earle was the leader of the women's Tektite II team.

Tektite II

In July 1970, Earle and her team of three scientists and an **engineer** entered the habitat. All had already gone through intensive training. Among other things, they had practiced using **rebreathers**. These are scuba-like tanks that recycle a diver's air.

The habitat, which sat on a **reef** in the Caribbean Sea, was small but comfortable. There were sleeping areas, a kitchen, and a laboratory. Special windows kept the stunning underwater neighborhood on view. The bottom had an opening that team members could easily exit to explore the warm, blue world around them.

The team spent as much time as possible in the water. Earle spent much of that time amazed. She noted that the habitat's outside was, "populated with settlers of colonies of algae, sponges, worms, and many other creatures." Earle was thrilled that the quiet rebreathers allowed her to hear natural underwater sounds, which would have been blocked by the bubbling sounds of a scuba tank.

Earle noticed that fish were curious about her too, but she was happier when they ignored her and went about their business. The long exposure underwater even allowed Earle to recognize the different personalities of individual fish.

Earle (black and white)
with three other members of
the Tektite II team.
Earle said nobody watched
the TV in the habitat, because
outside was the greatest show
on Earth.

Don't panic!

There was a frightening moment during the mission. Earle was exploring waters 1,000 feet (305 meters) away from the habitat when her rebreather failed. She could not breathe! An inexperienced diver might have panicked and risen quickly to the ocean's surface. But Earle knew a quick rise would likely give her the **bends**. It could even paralyze or kill her.

Instead, Earle signaled to her diving buddy, Peggy Lucas, the engineer on her team. Diving buddies stay close to each other underwater. Lucas quickly reached Earle. The two swam back together to the habitat, sharing air through Lucas' mouthpiece.

In the Tektite II habitat, Peggy Lucas shares research data with Earle.

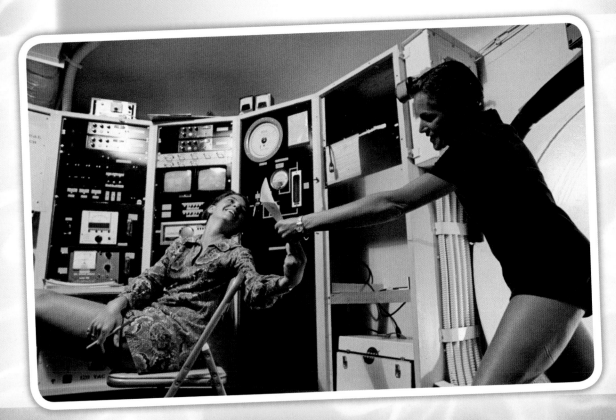

DID YOU KNOW?

When divers leave the water, their bodies must readjust to the lighter pressure on land. The longer a dive, the longer that adjustment takes. If divers rush the process, air in their lungs may expand too quickly. This can damage their lungs or send dangerous air bubbles into their bloodstream. Death or serious injury can occur. Long stays underwater, like the Tektite missions, require long adjustments to pressure changes.

Divers face another problem. Their bodies absorb nitrogen while breathing air from scuba tanks. If a diver rises too quickly in the water, nitrogen also creates bubbles in the body. This is called the bends. It too can be fatal.

A productive mission

The team's two weeks underwater were productive. Earle identified a wide variety of plant-eating fish. The team also found 154 kinds of algae in the habitat's liquid neighborhood. Of those, 26 **species** were not known to live in that part of the ocean world.

As their stay ended, the team members spent 21 hours in a sealed room called a decompression chamber. Here their bodies could readjust to breathing on land.

How Did Tektite Change Earle's Life?

The members of Earle's Tektite team were treated as heroes. They were honored in a Chicago parade and spoke to the U.S. Congress. They had lunch at the White House with First Lady Patricia Nixon and were presented Conservation Service Awards by the U.S. Secretary of the Interior.

Earle's team was the only Tektite II team honored this way. They knew it was because they were women. What they had done underwater was challenging, but not more challenging than what other teams did. Earle understood this and was always careful to accept honors on behalf of all the Tektite missions, not just her own. Yet she also believed the honors were a necessary step in making women's involvement in scientific projects as normal as men's.

DID YOU KNOW?

When Earle was first named team leader of the mission, a Boston newspaper ran the headline: "Beacon Hill Housewife to Lead Team of Female Aquanauts." The wording amused Earle. She did indeed live in Boston's Beacon Hill neighborhood, but she hoped that future headlines would describe her as a scientist, not a housewife.

In Her Own Words

Looking back on the Tektite II mission, Earle said:

"I'm changed forever because I lived underwater for two weeks in 1970. I wish that everybody could go live underwater if only for a day."

Earle (right) shows algae to another team member inside the habitat.

Becoming a public figure

Tektite II dramatically changed Earle's life. As mission leader, she was interviewed on TV talk shows. She was an entertaining guest who could talk easily about serious issues. Earle found ways to explain difficult scientific concepts to the public.

At first, Earle was uncomfortable in her new role as a celebrity. Like most scientists, she expected to live a life filled with serious study, not late night TV appearances. But Earle quickly realized that her TV interviews might help people worldwide understand the importance of healthy oceans.

TV was not the only way to reach people. Earle also wrote an article about Tektite for *National Geographic*, which more than 10 million people read. The article began Earle's lifetime relationship with the National Geographic Society as a writer, speaker, and film producer. The relationship helped make her a powerful spokesperson for the world's oceans.

Always exploring

Earle's new fame did not slow down her underwater explorations. At great risk and expense, she spent as much time in the ocean depths as possible.

In 1975 Earle led a research project in the underwater habitat Hydrolab. Among other things, she wanted to test the common scientific assumption that green algae could not grow more than 300 feet (91 meters) under the ocean's surface.

DID YOU KNOW?

Jacques Cousteau developed Conshelf, the first underwater habitat, in the 1960s. Starting in 1969, Hydrolab in the Bahamas hosted nearly 600 aquanauts on various missions over 15 years. Earle went on five missions there.

Submersibles like the *Johnson-Sea Link* take scientists to even deeper depths.

The Aquarius habitat still allows marine scientists to study the deep.

Johnson-Sea Link

A submersible named the *Johnson-Sea Link* visited Hydrolab. As with *Deep Diver*, its pilot could take Earle far underwater to explore. Earle hitched a ride and exited at 250 feet (76 meters), a risky depth for a diver breathing compressed air.

While exploring, Earle balanced herself on a rock wall and stared into the darkness below. She was tempted to swim down deeper but knew it would be foolishly dangerous. Near her, Earle spotted a tiny forest of unfamiliar green algae. She took a sample and later confirmed it was an undiscovered type. Was there more below?

Days later, the *Johnson-Sea Link* pilot took the submersible nearly 600 feet (183 meters) deep. He spotted more of the green algae! This was evidence that green algae could grow below a 300-foot (91-meter) depth. Later, Earle named the newly discovered algae *Johnson-sea-link profunda*, after the submersible.

How Far Has Earle Explored?

Earle's projects often combine exploration, scientific research, and her role as ocean protector. In 1975, with filmmaker Al Giddings, Earle investigated the deep waters of the Truk Lagoon in Micronesia. The lagoon had become a massive battleship graveyard after a 1944 World War II sea battle. Over time, the wrecks became artificial reefs.

Earle studied **coral** and plant life growing on those reefs. Earle and Giddings, supported by a small crew, made repeated dives into the wreckage. One of the divers, Kimiuo Aisek, lived on an island near Truk Lagoon. He witnessed the battle when he was just 17 years old. Aisek told Earle, "For more than two years afterward, oil from the ships and planes still covered the beaches and reefs, but the sea is healed now."

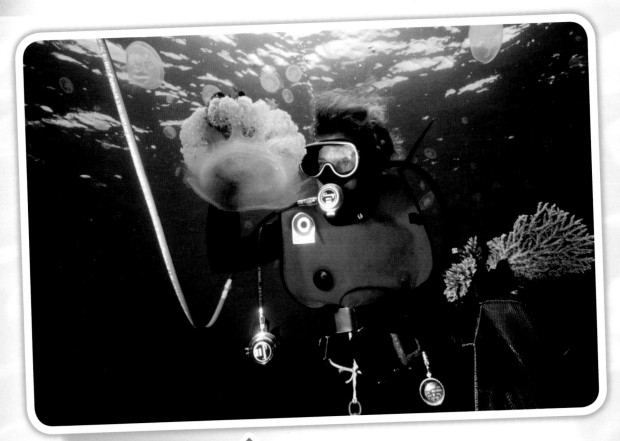

Earle studies a jellyfish in the Truk Lagoon.

Earle agreed with Aisek. But she also noted that 30 years after the battle, oil still leaked from the sunken ships. Earle wrote a 1976 article about these explorations for *National Geographic*. She concluded that algae had adopted the graveyard.

Learning about whales

In the 1970s, Earle joined Giddings and other scientists for a year-long study of humpback whales migrating between Hawaii and Alaska. The scientists recorded whale sounds and songs, eager to learn more about their communication. Earle spent much of her time swimming with the massive creatures. Humpback whales can be 40 feet (12 meters) long and weigh 40 tons (36 metric tons), yet Earle was constantly amazed by how graceful they were. She and the other divers got to know the individual whales they studied, naming two of their favorites Spot and Notchfin.

The team's whale adventures were documented in a film called *Gentle Giants of the Pacific* (1980). The documentary captures the beauty and importance of these creatures. It explains to the world the reasons to protect the oceans and its amazing creatures, particularly humpback whales.

DID YOU KNOW?

Whales are increasingly under threat from industry and **climate change**, as well as from hunting. In the last century, efficient ways of hunting dramatically reduced whale numbers. Some species were nearly wiped out. Seven of the 13 great whale species are still classified as **endangered** and vulnerable. Many people are working to protect these important animals.

Al Giddings

Al Giddings is a film producer, director, and cameraman. He is celebrated for documentary films about the sea. He has also been involved in the making of Hollywood movies, including *Titanic* (1997), *The Abyss* (1989), and *James Bond* movies.

Spreading the word

The film and the photographs that Giddings produced did more than document Earle's underwater feats. They also showed the world reasons to protect the oceans and their amazing inhabitants. Earle and Giddings still wanted to do more.

A spacesuit in the sea

In 1979 Earle and Giddings started on a risky new project. Earle planned to walk on the bottom of the sea in something called a **JIM suit**. Giddings would film the walk from a small submersible.

Earle bravely prepares to dive in the JIM suit.

DID YOU KNOW?

JIM is an atmospheric diving suit (ADS). These suits were first made in the 1930s to protect divers from the heavy pressure of water. The hard shell keeps the pressure in the suit the same as the pressure on land. The type of ADS that Earle used was developed in the 1960s for use in underwater construction. It was nicknamed after Jim Jarrett, a diver who had tested and used an ADS back in the 1930s.

Earle begins descent to the ocean floor, accompanied by a mini submarine.

The JIM suit looked like a spacesuit, but it was made of hard metal and ceramic (a clay-like substance). This meant it was heavier than anything an astronaut could use. The JIM suit weighed 1,000 pounds (454 kilograms) on land! It also had a rebreather system. This allowed the diver to stay underwater for hours before the air supply gave out.

With training, a skilled diver could move JIM's legs, arms, and claw-like hands. JIM was adapted to Earle's size and exploration goals. She then spent months training in the "walking refrigerator," as she called it. Earle also had long conversations with Giddings and a British marine engineer named Graham Hawkes about how dangerous her deep-sea walk might be.

A walk in the deep end

It took three attempts, but on October 19, 1979, Earle made history. The JIM suit, with Earle in it, was attached to a small submersible. They slowly descended to the ocean floor, a depth of 1,250 feet (381 meters). There Earle was released from the submersible and began to explore the bottom of the sea. She had radio communication with the submersible, but there was no tether connecting her to it. She was on her own. If Earle had trouble, there was no guarantee she could be rescued.

A record-setting walk

Earle was too delighted to be worried. Her two-and-a-half hour walk was a breathtaking wonder that few humans will ever experience. While Giddings filmed from the submersible, Earle gently poked and probed the undersea environment. At one point, she asked Giddings to turn off the submersible's lights. As her eyes adjusted to the darkness, Earle realized there were glowing creatures surrounding her that were **bioluminescent**. Although the walk was decades ago, Earle still gets chills when she describes what she saw that day.

Earle completed the deepest undersea walk ever made by any woman or man without a tether to the surface. Once again, Earle's bravery made headlines around the world. *National Geographic* later aired the camera footage of Earle's ocean floor adventure.

In Her Own Words

Earle described an amazing memory from her walk, saying:

"The most gentle nudge of my 'claw' provoked ring after ring of blue light to pulse from the point of contact down the full length of the coral. Small bright circles cascaded in neatly spaced sequences, fading to darkness after nearly a minute."

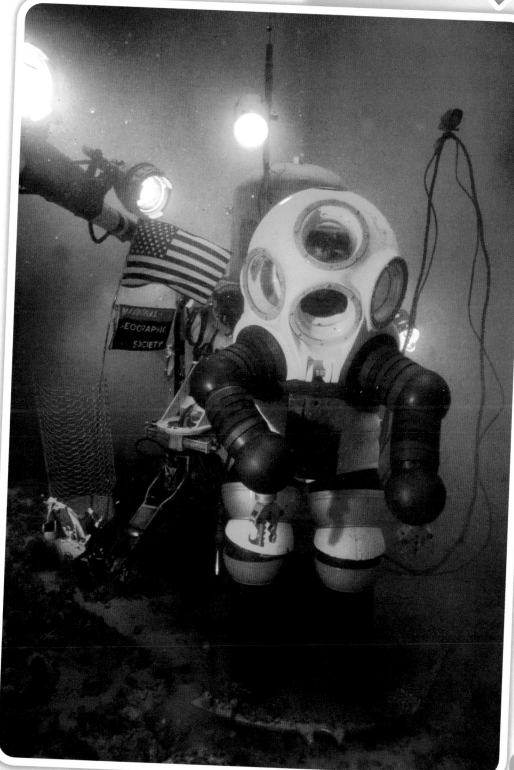

Earle walking on the bottom of the ocean.

How Have Earle's Explorations Helped to Protect the Oceans?

Earle wrote that after her record-setting sea walk, she was widely congratulated for her daring achievement. Yet she also realized that some people, including other scientists, thought her effort was more about setting records than conducting real research.

No blue, no green

Many people missed the point of her walk. So much of the ocean was unknown. Even today, more than 95 percent of the world's seas have not been explored. Yet the oceans and the life within them are vital to all life on Earth. Scientists must learn about and protect as much of the sea as possible. A favorite saying of Earle's is, "No blue, no green." In other words, if the ocean dies, Earth will die too.

The Mariana Trench is the deepest part of the world's oceans. Earle believes that investing in deeper and deeper exploration will reveal much more about the oceans, life on Earth, and even about space.

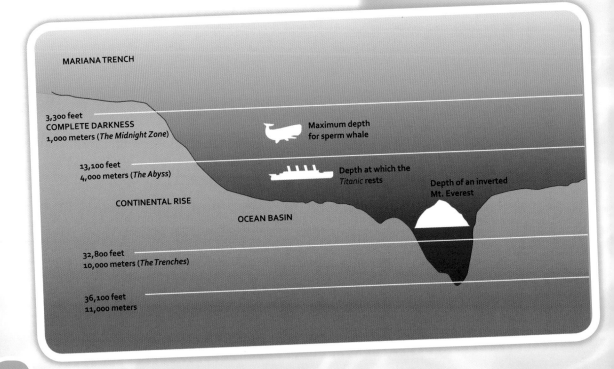

MARIANA TRENCH

3,300 feet
COMPLETE DARKNESS
1,000 meters (*The Midnight Zone*)

Maximum depth for sperm whale

13,100 feet
4,000 meters (*The Abyss*)

Depth at which the *Titanic* rests

Depth of an inverted Mt. Everest

CONTINENTAL RISE

OCEAN BASIN

32,800 feet
10,000 meters (*The Trenches*)

36,100 feet
11,000 meters

Earle and Graham Hawkes work together developing submersibles.

Earle wanted to encourage as much exploration as possible. In 1981 she joined with engineer Graham Hawkes in a somewhat unconventional effort for scientists. They created two companies, Deep Ocean Technology and Deep Ocean Engineering. These companies would make submersibles able to reach unexplored depths. Earle and Hawkes agreed this was one way to guarantee important research would continue.

DID YOU KNOW?

When Earle returned home from her record-setting JIM walk, she found that her children had teasingly placed a newspaper article on the refrigerator door. Its headline read: "Brave Mom's Historic Dive to the Bottom of the World."

Deep Rover

Combining Earle's underwater research experience with Hawkes' ocean engineering background, the two designed a one-person submersible called *Deep Rover*. However, it took years for them to find investors willing to provide the money necessary to build it.

In the meantime, Earle and Hawkes' companies successfully developed and sold remote-operated vehicles, called **ROVs**. The vehicles were controlled from the surface and used to inspect ocean **oil rigs** and other underwater structures.

By 1984 *Deep Rover* was being used for serious research, but the depths it could reach had not yet been tested. In 1985 Earle, Hawkes, and a third partner, Phil Nuytten, decided to push *Deep Rover* to the limit. They each took a turn guiding the submersible to a solo-diving record of 3,000 feet (914 meters).

The *Newtsub Deepworker 2000* is a more recent version of *Deep Rover*.

Earle was escorted by hundreds of dolphins as she began her descent into the ocean depths. Her excitement grew as *Deep Rover* successfully continued to dive deeper and deeper into the sea. Earle observed many varieties of life glowing in the dark, deep waters. She spotted tiny jellyfish, squid, and an octopus that had hitched a ride aboard *Deep Rover*.

Ocean litter

A bright-red object half-burried on the ocean floor caught Earle's eye. Using *Deep Rover's* outside-arms, she gently moved away the sand to identify the object. It was an empty soda can. For Earle, the soda can became an important symbol of how far human **pollution** had reached.

Deep Flight and more

Earle and Hawkes married in 1986. They went on to produce other notable submersibles.

Deep Flight was modeled after an airplane and designed to fly under the sea. Earle and Hawkes also worked on Ocean Everest, a project to build lightweight submersibles. Lighter weight meant they could reach even deeper parts of the oceans—deeper than Mount Everest is high!

In Her Own Words
Earle said:

"Debris from human activity litters the coastal areas of the world, but most of what goes into the sea remains unseen by those who put it there."

Hawkes also continued to design ROVs. The remote vehicles were used for everything, from underwater police searches to showing off the deep-water habitat created for EPCOT Center at Walt Disney World. Some ROVs were used for true scientific underwater exploration, which was Earle's real goal.

What Does Earle Worry About?

In 1989 a great environmental disaster occurred when the oil tanker *Exxon Valdez* ran aground on the coast of Alaska. The ship split open, pouring 11 million gallons (42 million liters) of oil into the sea. The gooey mess spread, covering the Alaskan coast.

Earle was called in to help find ways to heal the damaged environment. The devastation she witnessed deeply angered her. Earle was disheartened by what she called "the forever costs" of the catastrophe. She knew that much of what was destroyed would never come back.

In Her Own Words

Commenting on the *Exxon Valdez* oil spill, Earle said:

"It's an inexcusable outrage."

Alaskan coastline after the *Exxon Valdez* oil spill

Crews work to clean the Alaskan coast after the *Exxon Valdez* accident.

Deep matters

Earle's 1980s submersible work did not get in the way of her involvement in other issues. She continued her scientific research and was actively involved in the worldwide effort to protect oceans and ocean life. Earle debated with other scientists about the need to continue deep-water exploration. She argued that only five percent of the world's oceans have been explored. It is possible that two-thirds of Earth's plants and animals are under the seas, undiscovered.

An important new position

In 1990 U. S. President George H. W. Bush appointed Earle to a new job. Earle became chief scientist of the National Oceanographic and Atmospheric Administration (NOAA). She was the first woman to hold this position.

Dealing with disasters

The year before, the U.S. Congress had passed the Oil Pollution Act. This law was designed to avoid future accidental spills, like the *Exxon Valdez.* But the act could not prevent the deliberate oil-pollution disaster that occurred in 1991.

As the Persian Gulf War (1990–1991) ended, Iraqi army troops in Kuwait released 500 million gallons (1.9 billion liters) of oil into the Persian Gulf.

President Bush sent Earle to assess the damage. While she was there, oil wells in Kuwait went up in flames. The total devastation was unimaginable.

The widespread devastation of the Persian Gulf

しんかい6500

In later visits to Kuwait, Earle bravely scuba dived in oil-polluted waters to measure how much damage the disaster had caused.

The Japanese *Shinkai 6500* is lowered into the ocean.

The Persian Gulf oil spill occupied much of Earle's time at the NOAA. Political battles over important ocean and environmental issues consumed even more. In 1992 Earle resigned, frustrated over her inability to influence national environmental policy.

Achievements and challenges

Also in 1992, Earle made her deepest personal dive aboard a Japanese submersible, called the *Shinkai 6500*. She reached a depth of 13,065 feet (3,892 meters). That is 2.5 miles (4 kilometers) under the ocean's surface! Earle was thrilled with her achievement but irritated at the same time. Japan and many other nations had invested a lot of money into researching oceans. Earle felt the United States should do the same.

Defender of the seas

After Earle left the NOAA, she refocused on her goals of exploring and protecting Earth's oceans. At the end of 1992, Earle started her own company, DOER Marine, to produce submersibles. Earle was determined to continue and further human investigations of the seas.

In 1995 Earle published a book. *Sea Change: A Message of the Oceans* was a powerful argument for protecting the seas. The book was compared favorably to scientist Rachel Carson's books. Carson's most famous book, *Silent Spring*, has been credited with starting the environmental movement.

Opportunities and education

Earle gave up an active role in DOER Marine in 1998, when she was named a *National Geographic Explorer in Residence*. She was the first woman honored with this role. Since then, Earle has led *National Geographic*'s *Sustainable Seas Expeditions* program.

That same year, Earle was named *Time* magazine's first Hero for the Planet. These honors, along with many others, allowed Earle to continue her mission. She has convinced the world of the importance of the oceans and will forever protect what is living in them.

DID YOU KNOW?

Earle does not eat fish. She has told many interviewers that 95 percent of the large ocean fish that humans have enjoyed over the last century are gone.

"We are the ultimate **predators** of the oceans," she says.

Earle strongly makes the point that most fish humans eat have no careful efforts to guarantee their **sustainability**. She believes people should only eat the kinds of fish that can be raised on quality fish farms.

In 2010 the *Deepwater Horizon* oil rig exploded in the Gulf of Mexico. The explosion killed 11 workers and caused the second-largest oil spill in history. About 210 million gallons (795 million liters) of oil polluted the Gulf and its shores. Earle researched the cause of the disaster and studied the long-term effects. She testified before the U.S. Congress about what she had learned.

Many communities sued companies connected to *Deepwater Horizon* to pay for damages caused by the spill. One of the communities was Dunedin, Florida, where Earle had fallen in love with the ocean as a child.

Earle speaks on behalf of the oceans.

What Impact Has Earle's Work Had on Conservation?

As Earle has grown older, her energy has not weakened. She is still adding to her more than 7,000 hours exploring under the sea. In 2012 she made her 10th extended saturation dive.

Out of the water, Earle has had a direct influence on U.S. ocean policies. She continues her work for National Geographic and is also helping Google create detailed ocean maps.

Honors

Earle's efforts have been deeply appreciated. She has received more than 100 awards and honors for her courageous career. In 2000, the Library of Congress named her a Living Legend. In 2009, Earle was awarded the TED Prize. She used the $1 million that came with it to fund Mission Blue, an organization dedicated to supporting marine-protected areas.

Continuing her legacy

Mission Blue is one of the many ways Earle's **legacy** will live on. Another way is through her three children. Earle's oldest daughter runs DOER Marine. Her youngest daughter is a successful musician and experienced **oceanographer**. Much of her music reflects her interest in the seas. Earle's son works for California's Department of Fish and Game. In Earle's words, he "catches the bad guys" who fish or hunt protected wildlife.

Earle wants others to continue her legacy as well. *Facebook* users can "friend" her or *Mission Blue*. Earle has also written several books for children.

As she nears age 80, Sylvia Earle is still as fearless as ever. She says she will continue to dive as long as she breathes.

In Her Own Words

Earle had said:

"With every drop of water you drink, every breath you take, you're connected to the sea, no matter where on Earth you live."

Sylvia Earle standing beside her life's work and passion—the ocean.

Timeline

1935 Sylvia Earle is born in Gibbstown, New Jersey, on August 30.

1938 The Earle family moves to a farm near Paulsboro, New Jersey.

1948 The Earle family moves to a Gulf of Mexico waterfront property in Dunedin, Florida.

1952 Earle graduates from high school at age 16; makes her first breathing-assisted dive; learns scuba diving while taking a marine biology course taught by Harold Humm at Florida State University.

1955 Earle earns a bachelor's degree in marine botany from Florida State University.

1956 Earle earns a master's degree in marine botany from Duke University.

1964 Earle spends six weeks aboard the research ship *Anton Bruun* on a national science expedition in the Indian Ocean.

1965 Earle identifies an undiscovered algae and names it *Hummbrella hydra*, after Harold Humm; becomes resident director of the Cape Haze Marine Laboratory in Florida.

1966 Earle earns a doctorate degree from *Duke University*.

1968 In the submersible *Deep Diver*, Earle takes a 125-foot (38-meter) plunge to explore the ocean's floor in the Bahamas.

1969 Earle's study classifying types of algae in the Gulf of Mexico is published.

1970 Earle leads a team of four other women who live and work for 14 days in the Tektite II underwater habitat. Their achievement is widely reported and leads to Earle's growth as a national spokesperson on ocean-related science issues.

early 1970s Earle explores waters in the Indian Ocean and off of the Galapagos Islands, Panama, China, and the Bahamas.

1971 Earle's first article is published in *National Geographic*.

1975 Earle leads a research project in the underwater habitat Hydrolab, studying algae; investigates the waters of the Truk Lagoon in Micronesia with Al Giddings.

1977 Earle joins Giddings in a long-term project swimming with whales.

1979 In a JIM suit, Earle dives 1,250 feet (381 meters). She sets the record for the deepest dive without a tether.

1981 Earle and Graham Hawkes found Deep Ocean Technology to build vehicles that can explore ocean depths.

1984 Deep Ocean Technology designs *Deep Rover*, a one-person submersible.

1985 Earle takes a turn guiding *Deep Rover* down 3,000 feet (914 meters) underwater.

1990 U.S. President George H. W. Bush appoints Earle Chief Scientist of the National Oceanic and Atmospheric Administration (NOAA). Earle is the first woman to hold this position.

1992 Earle founds DOER Marine, a company that works to advance marine engineering; dives 13,065 feet (3,982 meters) in a Japanese submersible called the *Shinkai 6500*.

1995 Earle's book, *Sea Change: A Message of the Oceans*, is published.

1998 Earle is honored as Time magazine's first Hero for the Planet; is the first woman named as a National Geographic Explorer in Residence; leads the National Geographic Sustainable Seas Expeditions project.

2000 The Library of Congress names Earle a Living Legend.

2009 Earle wins the TED Prize; founds Mission Blue, an organization dedicated to protecting Earth by protecting its oceans.

Glossary

algae plantlike living things that live underwater and produce their own food

aquanaut person who explores under the oceans

bends illness divers experience when coming up too quickly from underwater depths

bioluminescent production of light by living organisms

carbon dioxide gas exhaled during respiration

climate change theory that human actions affect our planet's climate

compressed air air kept under pressure in a tank

conservation protection and care of an animal or place

coral hard, variously colored calcareous skeletons; living and dead coral make up coral reefs

endangered threatened with extinction

engineer person who designs and builds machines and structures

expedition trip or journey for a special purpose such as scientific study

food chain living things linked together because one uses another as food

habitat environment or place in which a plant or animal naturally lives

ichthyologist scientist who studies fish

JIM suit underwater suit that looks like a spacesuit, but is made of very heavy materials; it has a rebreather system and maneuverable "arms" and "legs" for the diver to control

legacy story or gift that is left behind for future generations

marine relating to the sea or found in the sea

marine biology science that studies life in the sea and other bodies of water

marine botanist scientist who studies plants and plantlike living things that live in the water

oceanographer scientist who studies oceans and the living things within them

oil rig large structure used to drill into the ground or under the seas to find oil

photosynthesis process in which green plants use light, carbon dioxide, and water to make their own food; a by-product of the process is oxygen

pioneer first person to do something; also, the act of doing something first, such as using scuba equipment to explore the ocean

pollutant something that makes air, water, or soil harmful to humans and other living things

pollution presence of a substance or substances that are harmful or poisonous

predators animals that hunt other living organisms

rebreather underwater scuba-like device that recycles and purifies a diver's air to allow a longer dive

reef ridge of coral, sand, or rocks near or above the water's surface

ROV remote-operated vehicle that can be controlled from above the seas and be used to inspect things underwater

saturation dive long-term stay underwater that allow divers' bodies to more easily recover from undersea exploration

scuba dive swim underwater with an air tank, mask, breathing apparatus, and fins

species group of living things that are related to each other

specimen sample of a type of something; a rock is a kind of specimen

submersible craft designed to work deep under the sea; it is usually tethered to either another ship or a platform above

sustainability supports long-term ecological balance

Tektite underwater laboratory

tether something such as a rope that limits the movement of something else; also, to prevent something from moving too far

zoologist scientist who studies animals

Find Out More

Books

Earle, Sylvia. *Dive!: My Adventures in the Deep Frontier*. Washington, D.C.: National Geographic Society, 1999.

Earle, Sylvia. *Sea Change: A Message of the Oceans*. New York: G. P. Putnam's Sons, 1995.

Gray, Susan Heinrichs. *Oceanography: The Study of Oceans* (True Book). New York: Children's Press, 2012.

Sandler, Michael. *Oceans: Surviving in the Deep Sea* (X-Treme Places). New York: Bearport, 2006.

Websites

aquarius.fiu.edu
Visit the website of the Aquarius Underwater Laboratory, the underwater laboratory that Sylvia Earle lived in for a while and later worked to save. The website shows how it is used.

www.google.com/earth/explore/showcase/ocean.html
"Ocean" in Google Earth explores the mysteries and geography of the oceans. Earle narrates and explains much of what is shown.

mission-blue.org
This is the inspiring website for Mission Blue, the organization that Earle founded after she won the TED Prize.

ocean.nationalgeographic.com/ocean/
The *National Geographic* website is one of the Internet's best places to learn about Earth's oceans and the varieties of life within them.

DVDs

Oceans, Volume 1. New York: PBS, 2010.

Whales: An Unforgettable Journey. Burbank, California: SlingShot Entertainment, 2001.

Places to Visit
The Florida Aquarium
701 Channelside Drive
Tampa, Florida 33602

www.flaquarium.org

Visitors to the Florida Aquarium will enjoy learning about life in and near the oceans. The aquarium is a two-hour drive from Dunedin, Florida, where Sylvia Earle lived as a child.

Monterey Bay Aquarium
886 Cannery Row
Monterey, California 93940

www.montereybayaquarium.org

The mission of this beautiful aquarium is to inspire visitors to appreciate and conserve ocean life.

What Can I Do?
Sylvia Earle would like your help in keeping the ocean blue and the Earth green. Here are three things you can do to help:

- Only eat fish grown on fish farms. Eating fish that have to be caught in the wild, like tuna, reduces the world's fish supply. The ocean's health depends on fish. Our health depends on the oceans.

- Do not buy jewelry or products made from coral, sharks, turtles, or other vital members of the undersea environment.

- Use as few plastic products as possible and recycle what you do use. Too much plastic winds up in the ocean and harms ocean life.

Index